Love &Such

Maxine Brothers

Copyrighted Material

Love & Such
Copyright ©2008 by Maxine Brothers

All rights reserved. No part of this publication may be reproduced,
stored in a retrieval system, or transmitted in any form
by any means-electronic, mechanical, photocopy, recording, or
any other- except for brief quotation in printed reviews with
prior permission of the publisher.

ISBN: 978-0-615-25274-2

Special Dedications

Thank you to my Family, Biological Family, Spiritual Family, and all the Family I met along the way. Thank you for keeping me grounded, for keeping me focused, keeping me in your prayers and most importantly supporting my efforts. To the loves of my life Dejah, Danah, Tailon, Tywon, Brooklynn and Ayanna, know that there is nothing that auntie will not do for you babies. Love you forever and ever.

Table of Contents

6.................................**Loves Gentle Strokes**
   7...............................Beautiful
   8...............................More Than The Skin I'm In
      9.............................It's Morning
      10...........................Lay Beside Me
      11...........................Nothing But Truth
      12........................... Suddenly
      13...........................I Called Him Love

14.................................**Loves Turbulence**
   15.............................Confused
   16.............................Message To Love
   17.............................Shades of Us
   18.............................The Real Thing Confused
   19.............................In Too Deep

20.................................**Things I Learned Along The Way**
   21.............................Nothing Better
   22.............................I Will Gladly Tell You
   23.............................Options
   24.............................Statistic
   25.............................Alone I Stand
   26.............................Indivisible X's 3

27.................................**And Such**
   28.............................Chocolate Honey
   29.............................I'm Not Listening
   30.............................Jealous
   31.............................The Gift of Imagination
   32.............................Keeping up with Yesterday
   33.............................Niggas For Sale
   34.............................A Song For Ruby B
   35.............................Apologies(Torn)
   36.............................Appreciated
   37.............................My M.A.C
   38.............................My Last Breath
   39.............................Nobody's Nigga
   40............................. Deeper
   41.............................Why Didn't You Stay
   42.............................Think First
   43.............................Nightmare or Sign
   44.............................Welcome To America
   45.............................Devoted
   46.............................Gone(A Short Story About Love Lost)

And now Love and Such

Enjoy!!!!!

Loves Gentle Strokes

BEAUTIFUL

I imagine you like a canvas, ready to be painted with fresh oils, to caress the inner twining of my henna paper.

I see you in bright oranges, deep reds, and strong blues.

I see you with the potential of a Monet, but with the personality of a Picasso.

I imagine you deep with meaning, made with strokes of simplicity, you are beautiful and yet an original.

I imagine you with heavens and earth painted on your very being.

I see you dark and yet full of light.
I imagine you, you are beautiful.
I imagine you, you are beautiful.

You
Are
Beautiful.

MORE THAN THE SKIN I'M IN

I'm praying that he sees more than the skin I'm in.
I struggle with whether I should bear myself to him and
catch his attention, or should I let him get to know my inner beauty?

Inside I scream.

I'm more than a pretty face,
with a thin waist and a wide behind.
Yet, no one hears me and even if I had said it out loud,
what would it matter to anyone but me?

It seems while under all my layers, I may be more;
but maybe it's too many layers to adore.
Yet, I pray that he sees more than the skin I am in.
Maybe I flash him with my intelligence, my thoughts
of past and present remnants, share a proverb or two,
or do things the less curvy will not do.

Nothing obscene because I am a Queen.
With thick proportions,
No mind distortions,
Just want to be seen.

IT'S MORNING

I slowly caress your skin, sun toasted black.
Touching your soft lips as you touch me back.
Slowly, you kiss me; it's as sensuous as your touch.
My mind slips into thoughts of why I love you so much.
Oh, how many ways can I count why I need you here,
Running your fingers down my spine, as I enjoy having you near.
Never letting your love escape me,
I close my eyes and hope what's in my heart you can see.
Now, the sunlight is shining on our face,
Glowing through us, it seems, as we embrace.
I touch your face to let you
Know it's you that I adore.
I'm into you
And now its morning.

LAY BESIDE ME

Lay beside me, caress and kiss me.
Hold my hand and squeeze me.
Let's make love,
Sex will come later.
I want to know about the love you have;
Become intimate with my mind.
Wrap me up
In your conversation.
Make me want you,
Need you.
Grow with me.
Build with me.
Rule beside me.
Pray with me.
Let's explore mental ecstasy.
I want to become high on your love,
And not confused by our lust.
Be my King
And I will be your Queen.
I want to know about the faith you have.
Let's serve God as a union because without him,
there can't be any us.
I want to love you as I love my body,
So there can't be any harm.
I want to want you
Not just in the bedroom, but in my life.
Be my man
And I'll be your wife.
Let's be exclusive
And I promise life will never be dull,
Not for a day, but for a lifetime;
Not to the extent of your lifeline, but forever.
Let's be together.
Lay beside me
And let's just be.

NOTHING BUT TRUTH

He allows me to bear my Truths, ugly and unaware.
On my shoulders <u>Nothing</u> but Truth, tearful and overwhelmed.
See, he allows me to bear my Truths, of yesterdays events,
of the things I resent <u>Nothing</u> but Truth.
Accosted and ashamed, bear Truths on my frame, as long as it's Truth.
See, he understands that <u>Nothing</u> is worse than changing the person
without changing the problem, and without Truth, how can you solve them?
See, he allows me to bear my Truths—soul scarred, yet dreams unmarred.
Truth is ugly and unaware, on my heart, weighing me down heavily.
Yet, I bear these Truths, to be self evident, of the years and tears I've spent,
Of yesterday's events, of the things I resent.
With him, I don't have to pretend.
And that's the Truth.

Suddenly

Never was one to believe in love at first sight.
Never was one to want to make love the first night.
And suddenly, there you were
In my world, in my heart, and in my bed.
I fell for you just when I thought love was dead.
Suddenly,
I wanted to be yours and yours only.
I loved you so suddenly.
With that first glance
First words, first smile,
Yes Suddenly.
Never been one to believe in love at first sight.
Never been one to want to make love on the first night and yet
Suddenly,
You had me
Wrapped up and willing.
I was yours for the keeping,
But you were never going to be mine for the taking.
My heart is suddenly breaking
Because suddenly it was morning,
And you are gone.

I CALLED HIM LOVE

He was a like a cool breeze on a summer's day.
His mind, body, and soul refreshed me in a sensuous way.
He could move mountains even though he was only a pebble.
He was well bred, but had the air of a rebel.
He was gentle, kind,
sweet, divine,
strong, sensuous,
and could do things with his mind.
He was caring but stern,
And as gentle as a dove.
I didn't have him long,
But I called him, love.

Love's Turbulence

CONFUSED

I hate you,
But can't stand to be without you.
Promises you make, but all I can do is doubt you.
Want to believe your love is real,
But I don't know how to.
Can't trust you,
But some how I still want to. Want you out of my life, but I don't know
how-to keep living without you.
Can't eat,
Can't sleep,
And all I do is think about you.
Can't breath cause when you leave,
All I want to do is follow you.
When I say I hate you,
I really mean I love you,
I hate that I'm co-dependant on you
For the attention that you give only when you want to.
Can't believe that in my dreams I want to marry you;
Because when you're around I can't stand you,
But I can't stand to be without you.

MESSAGE TO LOVE

Love, where have you been?
Just a few months ago, you were my summertime friend.
Now, winter has rolled around and you are nowhere to be found.
Thought I saw you the other day love,
but it was just a reflection in a puddle on the ground.
Just the other day love, I thought I heard you calling my name.
With you out of my life, I think I'm going insane.
Since you've been gone, my heart's been playing tricks on my mind,
been messing with my eyes and the tears that I cry.
Love, without you there is no me.
I'm slipping, I'm falling love, come back to me.
Love, where did you go?
I'm searching for you once again, love, in people I don't know.
At one point, love, we were on the same page;
how many kids we wanted, how we wanted to spend our old age.
But love has gone and love has walked out the door.
Got to change the welcome mat.
Love doesn't live here any more.

SHADES OF US

Our love colored in red. Caliente.
warm as the sun, like two flaming habanero peppers dipped in bronze.
You were my King and you took care of our home
even when the remnants of us turned blue, cold as ice.
However, that was the sacrifice made for two flaming lovers as dark as a spade.
Our shades became one, impenetrable to the sun.
We never felt its heat; for I was your shade and you were my cool breeze,
and when the sun seemed to fade, you were my blanketa grande` on a winter's day.
When I was lost in the dark, you were my iridescent flame
that flickered constantly,
reminding me of how love is supposed to be.
Sometimes, I still feel you near me.
Now, your love has turned black never again to turn red.
A decision was made, and I still struggle with it in my head.
You were my love, but you are no longer here.
However, forever I will hold the shades of you, shades of me, shades of we, near.

THE REAL THING CONFUSED

Our love, not to be confused with the real thing, you said felt real to me.
But as mirages they don't last, and it's hard for me to breathe because I saw it coming.
And while the existence of you in my life was for a short stint in time,
I found myself needing you.
Needing you like refugees need stable shelter.
Needing you like the survivors of the tsunami need fresh water.
Needing you like an embryo needs nine months to grow to ensure it's able to survive birth.
Needing you like Mexican immigrants need to work.
And I ache for the millions of times you lied to me,
confessing your undying love under crescent moons and over desert sands.
But our love is not to be confused with the real thing that you said became a reality,
not just in my head, but in my heart.
And while in your reality we never existed,
My heart continuously beats to a steady rhythm of needing you
Like Afghanistan needs peace,
Like an insomniac needs to sleep, and
Like war needs to cease.
I am needing you like I need air to breath.
Our love, not to be confused with the real thing, you said felt real to me.

IN TOO DEEP

Not a lover of him, but I kept you close as kin.
You were a confidant, a mentor, a friend, but my values changed, and you are no longer down.
I wonder why I assumed you would not make me cry?
Now I love him with exclusive devotion and you think I am still coming back; what gives you that notion?
I love you different than I used too. I am no longer that friend that you thought you knew.
See, you are in too deep with your own thinking.
You assume I could love him, with us continually speaking,
but a lover of you could not be a lover of him.
Even though you were a mentor, a confidant, a friend.
See, I am in too deep with this newfound love.
I love the one who created the heavens above and to him he receives my full attention.
Oh, did I forget to mention?
I am in to deep and there will be no turning back.
Knowing that he is the answer to all my problems and me not trying to solve them, I cannot get down like that.
This is where I say goodbye because this is hurting, I can see.
I feel for you love, but I am in too deep.

Things I have learned along the way.

NOTHING BETTER

Nothing like a morning kiss,
Nothing like being able to reminisce.
Nothing like morning dew,
Nothing like grandma's stew.
Nothing like being held,
Nothing like the way you smell.
Nothing like late night talks,
Nothing like midday walks.
Nothing like first-year snow,
Nothing like pressing cookie dough.
Nothing like being free to speak,
Nothing like building you up when you are weak.
Nothing like singing a song,
Nothing like righting a wrong.
Nothing like being free to give,
Nothing like having a life to live.
Nothing like new sights to see,
Nothing like being free.
There's nothing better than life,
Nothing better.

I WILL GLADLY TELL YOU

They say things happen for a reason. Could it be that we are asking for a sign, and we just received it just at the wrong season? I take my experiences as a mode of teaching.

I will gladly tell you of my life and my struggles, but will you listen? Will you listen when I tell you that the life of being a thug, will lead you to a life of misery? Will you listen when I tell you that having no vision leaves you blind, and being guided by someone who can barely see?

I will gladly tell you of the beatings I took, from these want-to-be crooks, because I'm a strong black woman and gave them dirty looks.
But will you listen?
I'm not just talking to hear myself speak. My life was rough; I survived so I'm here to teach.

ARE YOU LISTENING NOW?

Will you listen when I tell you that nobody will love you more than you love yourself? Or will you continue to run with your crew, because they say they love you, and will be there when you need help?

Will you listen when I tell you that a child will not make things ok? A baby will not make the current love of your life stay.

Will you listen to the stories of those before me and take them as lessons learned? History repeats itself in a 360 motion, just as the world turns.

ARE YOU LISTENING NOW?

I know you hear me but I want you to understand,
And please don't tell me I'm tripping.
I will gladly tell you of my life struggles, but will you listen?

OPTIONS

Having the option to leave does not making leaving an option.
As I watch out my window, I struggle to hold back the tears, the hatred the fears.
That spin in my mind that intertwines with the knowledge that I spit, and some cannot get with.
Or have the capacity to even converse with me about the days of Martin and Muhmia, Malcolm, and Gandhi who fought for me, and I couldn't understand until I had to fight for the next man. And it scares me in the night to the point that I want to take flight, but
Having the option to leave does not make leaving an option.
As I preach to those who have yet to lose the eye of ignorance, I get frustrated.
And in my frustrations, I pray to my Father for the strength to carry on and be strong, and the power to admit when I'm wrong and keep a song.
But the stress I feel makes me want to walk out the door in the middle of the night and take flight, but
Having the option to leave does not make leaving an option.
See, these young girls think that walking these streets with these ripped up sheets and these wild hair do's, and these hooker-type moves make them feel like they got a groove, when actually, they should be in school getting educated.
But the truth got faded between the music they listen to and getting their hair braided.
And those who should have been teaching weren't there; but not me because,
Having the option to leave does not make leaving an option.

STATISTIC

He knows that if he dies, he's just a statistic.
If he lies, he isn't with it.
Dreams unrealized,
Y'all don't get it.
He's a struggling hustler not really into the street life.
Selling what he can just to be rich with his hood wife.
Y'all not hearing me.
If he dies, he's just a statistic.
If he lies, he isn't with it.
Out here, he's committing crimes just to make it.
He's not really of the criminal type,
But he doesn't know any better.
Brother got hoop dreams,
Got to make that cheddar.
He's got five kids, four baby mothers,
And had almost every STD known to man
'Cause the kid don't use any rubbers.
He thinks he's living but he doesn't know what that means.
Makes a couple of G's in the hood,
And now he's down with the team.
But he's on the road to death, not realizing he's only a statistic.
Dreams unrealized,
Two shots to the chest.
And that train OOPS, he must have missed it.
All it took was misdirection and no education.
Now, he's a statistic and his boss just replaced him with another young dreamer,
Understanding the same thing.
If he dies, he's just a statistic.
If he lies, he isn't with it.
Dreams unrealized,
Young brother, when you gone get it?

Statistic

ALONE I STAND

I'm my own mind and my own spirit when I write my rhymes, and I spit my lyrics.
I have these feelings that make me warm when I'm feeling cold.
All my strength goes with being bold, when the earth gets quiet and I'm all alone, I school these chiefs to lies untold, that needs to be heard cause truth is better than empty words.
Now I rest my mind and try to sleep, but my other side needs to take a drink, because all this stress isn't good for me.
Where I once was one, now I think like three; my mind keeps spinning constantly.
With every turn, my emotional scars cause emotional burns
and my soul is tortured, but I keep it tight.
My sanity is questioned with every night, but I don't listen to those who judge and cause problems on every land.
No need for armies because alone, I stand.

INDIVISIBLE X'S 3

I waken every morning and place my problems on a shelf,
There's no reason why I should keep accosting myself.
I'm a strong, black woman indivisible X's 3, full of hope.
STRONG BLACK WOMAN YEAH THAT'S ME.
I work everyday and I take care of home,
I know how to keep a man, but I can stand on my own.
I'm a strong, black woman indivisible X's 3, full of pride.
STRONG BLACK WOMAN YEAH THAT'S ME.
I'll accept you into my heart, but I'm strong enough to let you go.
My pride doesn't get scarred just to let you know.
I'm a strong, black woman indivisible X's 3 full of love,
STRONG BLACK WOMAN YEAH THAT'S ME.
My views never distorted by another's opinion,
There's only enough room for one ruler amongst this queen's dominion.
I'm a strong, black woman indivisible X's 3, full of wisdom.
STRONG BLACK WOMAN YEAH THAT'S ME.
My battle scares are many and yet there are more to come,
I fear no man!!!!
For the battle has just begun.
I'm a strong, black woman indivisible X's, 3 full of faith.
STRONG BLACK WOMAN YEAH THAT'S ME.
Strong because I don't know how to else to be,
STRONG BLACK WOMAN INDIVISIBLE X'S 3
STRONG BLACK WOMAN YEAH THAT'S ME.

And Such

CHOCOLATE HONEY

They call me Chocolate Honey,
The original Playboy bunny;
The one that got Luke giving up all his money.
Yeah, I see y'all broads think it's funny,
But y'all don't know how many times I played the game.
Yeah that's me, winner one and only.
See, your man knew how many times it took
With every twist of my hips,
He didn't have to take a second look.
You acting like you still don't know,
Maybe Pimpstress diva or number one man stealer for sho.
But a man stealer I ain't for real,
Can't keep what don't want to be kept.
Baby, you don't know the deal.
See, I'm chocolate from my head to my toes,
And sweet down to the middle of my soul.
So while he asking me for a chance,
You'll be looking for romance.
I'm about to make a dash with his cash,
Naw, I don't love that fool,
He just a tool for my survival,
All the while making you haters, my rival.
You can snicker but it really isn't all that funny,
Let me introduce myself
My name is Chocolate Honey.

I'm Not Listening

Don't shout
It's not that I
Didn't hear you,
I wasn't listening.
And what I did catch,
Wasn't worth my attention.
Oh, did I mention
I'm not listening?
You're giving birth to
Empty thoughts and
Oh, I missed the point.
Not that I don't get it,
But it's just that I don't care.
See, I'm looking for
New ideas and
Fresh sentiments,
But you're caught up in
Yesterday so
Once again,
I'm not listening.
Can't be caught up in reminiscing
of old ideas and
Mundane conversation.
See, there you go again shouting;
I can hear you,
I'm just not listening.
No need to focus
On the things you're saying,
Because what you are saying means nothing.
I'm sorry means nothing to me.
Can't entertain the
Simple talk or idol gossip.
Sounds like
Blah blah blah.
Oops, I know that you're just venting,
But I'm sorry; I'm not listening.

Jealous

Look at you trying to steal my shine.
You're jealous because I sip the best, and you can't get a bottle of $4.99 wine.
Look at you trying to walk like me, talk like my baby that's called stalking, you see.
Don't be jealous cause my flow's my own.
You're trying to strip me of my title because your words are dry as bones.
Now you gritting ha ha what you don't like my tone?
I let you sit in on my sessions, I gave you a few lessons,
had you under my thumb, and gave you my blessings.
And this is how you repay me? Smile up in my face but when I turn my back, you try to slay me? Awe, you thought you was slick trying to bust my flow.
But I bounced back quick, knowing without me, there is no you.
I put you on the map and then your status grew, but
Before me no one wanted to here you.
You were a nobody,
A voiceless face in the crowd,
And you know all I'm saying is true.
See, all the times you got booed
and laughed at,
What did you think that everyone is just rude?
It was me that got you accepted.
Better check yourself or find yourself disrespected.
Or maybe, I should put you out of your misery now;
Without me, there is no flow and you have no style.

THE GIFT OF IMAGINATION

See, I have this imagination that takes me from the plantation to the fox five station and back.
It sounds whack, but I see things before you can paint it, not the mundane, but something out of this world, not a crazy girl, just able to see with my third eye.
I know why the caged bird cries and not sings; they clipped his wings and made him a slave.
Yes, in the land of the free and the home of the brave, but I see him in colors of freedom.
Not red, white, and blue, but the color of every man on this land the colors of me and you.
I imagine things before they can ever be explained. Many of my folks complain because before they know the question, I know the answer, because I have already seen it, contemplated the joys and pain of it, the sun and rain of it, and while it doesn't make me sick, it makes me tired.
Not always inspired, but I continue to imagine that the best scenario pumps loud in my brain like a stereo with beautiful rays of possibility.

I hold no hostility. This is a gift, a gift of imagination.

Keeping up with yesterday

He's a constant reminder of
All the things that I want to be,
Minus all the I can't do's
With a side order of possibilities.
He worries about what may come,
And it traps him in the here and now.
It makes him feel like there's no hope
To be all he can, but he can't see how.
He struggles with the idea of
Failure, so he won't try;
Not without a guarantee,
Or a real reason why.
He could be as free as
A bird without a proverbial limb,
But his wings were clipped by his fear,
So now his future looks grim.
He's only a shadow of
The man he could definitely be,
But he's stifled by
The reality of uncertainty.
But with all that he can do,
He's all that I strive to be,
And all that I want to do,
If only I could just believe.
See, we suffer from the same desire
Or the sufferable mentality
Beyond all the lack of faith,
And little idiosyncrasies;
But with all that he hopes to be,
It helps to keep my hope alive,
That one day we'll be strong enough
To make our dreams arrive.

NIGGA'S FOR SALE

UP FOR SALE, GOT ME A NIGGER WOMAN
NOT TOO EDUCATED, FAIRLY SCRAWNY,
BUT GOT BABY-MAKING HIPS.
LOVES TO STRIP
DOESN'T CARE TO READ OR TEACH HER SEED,
BUT SMOKES WEED.
ASPIRES TO DO NOTHING MORE THAN TO MAKE ENDS MEET.
SHE'S HARD TO UNDERSTAND WHEN SHE SPEAKS;
IT'S NOT ENGLISH AT ALL, SOMETHING THEY CALL EBONICS,
BUT IT'S NOT DUE TO SMOKING CHRONIC.
SHE'LL DO WHATEVER YOU TELL HER FOR THAT DOLLAR,
SHE'S ON THE SELLERS BLOCK
GOING TO THE HIGHEST BIDDER.
YOU COULD MAKE HER YOUR VIDEO VIXEN,
BUT SHE'LL NEVER PLAY THE VICTIM.
SHE GOT MAD SKILLS, BUT THEY DON'T EQUATE TO HIGHER
EDUCATION.
SHE GOT A FEW KIDS, BUT YOU COULD TRAIN EM.
HER LITTLE BOY WILL GROW UP TO BE A THREE-TIME FELON
FOR A LITTLE GUN PLAY, BUT A LOT OF DRUG SELLIN.
HIS ONLY MALE ROLE MODELS ARE ON B.E.T.
SELLING CRACK PIPE RHYMES AND
GHETTO SUPA STAR DREAMS.
HER LITTLE GIRLS ARE GOING TO BE JUST LIKE HER:
UNEDUCATED AND UNKNOWING OF THEIR SELF WORTH,
AND GIVING BIRTH TO LITTLE NIGGAS JUST LIKE THEM.
WHEN WILL THIS VISCIOUS CYCLE END?
WHOLE FAMILIES UP FOR SALE
AND THEY DON'T EVEN KNOW IT.
SEE, THERE'S A MARKET FOR NIGGA'S

ACEY SAID IT
BUSCHES ANCESTORS BREAD IT
AND THEY REFUSE TO LET IT GO.
NOT ENOUGH ASPIRING DOCTORS,
BUT PLENTY ASPIRING VIDEO HOES
OR WANNA BE GANGSTAS
YELLING CHECK, CHECK OUT MY MELODY.
I SAID I GOT THIS NIGGA FAMILY Y'ALL
GOING TO THE HIGHEST BIDDER.
THEY DON'T COST MUCH,
NOT EVEN SEVEN FIGURES.
GOT NIGGAS FOR SALE Y'ALL
GOT NIGGAS FOR SALE.
GOT NIGGAS FOR SALE Y'ALL
GOT NIGGAS FOR SALE.

A SONG FOR RUBY B

I want to write her a song of beautiful harmonies.
Like her welcoming smile, her loving style,
And the way she used to cook.
A song for the hugs she gave,
For the times she prayed,
And how you knew she cared just by a look.
I want to write her a melody.
So beautiful,
Like her understanding,
Never demanding,
Just mild and meek.
She was a great lady,
Sweeter than Sadie,
She was Ruby B.
Called many a name,
Never showed her pain,
And kept her chin up high.
Always gave a helping hand,
And that's where the virtues lie.
A song for Ruby B,
A song to sing.
Of all the great memories it will bring,
For all those she left behind,
I want to write her a song,
A song for Ruby B.

APOLOGIES (TORN)

I am sorry he made you cry.
I am sorry he felt he had to lie.
I am sorry he hid you in shame.
I am sorry you ever knew his name.
I am sorry for the truths I never told.
I am sorry that to have his love, you had to sell your soul.
I am sorry that his untruth wasn't evident.
I am sorry he'll never repent.
I am sorry that he wasted your time.
I am sorry that with him, you went blind.
I am sorry that your love went in vain.
I am sorry that he caused you so much pain.
I am sorry that sadly, you can't make it end
I am sorry that I called him a friend

I am sorry.

© Maxine Brothers

Appreciated

I reached my arms out and then I knew,
You reached back you love me too.
You took me in your arms and let me know,
That whenever I needed love,
This is where I should go.
You did things for me my own mother wouldn't,
And that's why I appreciate you,
You never said you couldn't.
We always talked about the things we wanted to do,
We intertwined conversation-wise
And that's why I appreciate you.
This is not a love ballad,
Because our love could never be dated.
This is to let you know, you are appreciated.

MY M.A.C

Its morning, I shower, dress and I reach for the concealer to cover up my battle scars
Too deep really to be seen by any man,
But my Mac allows for me to create the illusion of beauty,
When every thing I feel is ugly.
M A C
Making
Another
Change
Like a chameleon
So that no one see's how deeply
I have been affected
Daily Reflected
On the past so that it stays out of my future.
Wounds so deep I think I need a suture
Or maybe some stitches to mend this broken soul
So I layer on my foundation
NW45
Stands for Nothing Really to anyone but me
But as for me it stand for Not Without a fight
Never again, will allow someone to touch me so deeply that I can't or I refuse to recover from the loss of them.
Never again, will I give my all to someone, that I know is not willing to spend the span of two life times with me in his arms.
Never again, will I my give body to someone who does not love my body as he loves his.
Not without a fight that is.
So
I add eyeliner to make my eyes look deep and shadow so that there appears to be life in them
Do not want anyone to see that am Just a shadow of the woman I was in my Early 20's
A ghost really.
I look in the mirror to add the finishing changes
And thank the makers of my makeup
For the ability to hide what no one should ever see
I grimace at the thought of it not being permanent
See, tomorrow it will be morning and I will be reaching for my concealer, to cover up these battle scars to deep to be seen by any man.

My Last Breath

I'm taking my last breath and it hurts. I'm leaving this earth no longer a mass of energy; I remember when I had a ball of it contained within me. Now, I lay inside my bed with memories of yesterday in my head, and I wish that yesterday would have never left. Because today I'm here alone dealing with my death and I start to cry, wondering why I have wasted time.
Wanting and waiting
Wanting and waiting
Wanting and waiting
When I should have been going and getting all of the things of my desire instead, I have nestled and saved for a rainy day. It's raining now and I'm lying here taking my last breath, and it hurts.

NOBODY'S NIGGA

Wasn't raised in the fields
Picking cotton, you understand,
don't answer to any Masah
Or any Uncle Tom field hand.
Got more education
than my fathers from before,
So I won't take being called
Someone's nigga anymore.
Don't want to hear it amongst friends,
That word I do despise.
This word not meant to be harmful, Please,
Don't believe my brother's lies.
I'm not ignorant nor do I act as such,
Being a nigga means being less,
and I can't take that punch.
The word nigga was meant to berate,
belittle, and to teach hate.
So as a people, why do we say it to our friend's and family and
even our mates?
I'm nobody's nigga,
I say it again.
Don't pull that verbal trigger,
You might blow off you own hand.
I'm nobody's nigga,
Not meant to be a comedy.
I am not anybody's nigga,
So don't say that to me.

DEEPER

As I look at you,
I try to look deeper into your soul.
I try to envision your dreams,
Your story untold.
And as I dig deeper,
I see you for who I think you are
A shallow, vain, shadow of a man
Who thinks he's a star.

Yet, I dig deeper to find out why you are that way,
In all the confusion I forget why I stay.
Then I dig deeper and you show me
Another side of you.
A person that loves and feels a man that is real,
And so I dig deeper
Because while figuring you out,
I lost myself.
Or maybe I just decided to put me on the shelf.
You helped me find my way; no longer a self happiness seeker.
How glad I am that I decided to dig deeper.

WHY DIDN'T YOU STAY?

You said you would love me always,
And hold my hand across desert sands.
You said you would hold me forever,
And now your love is no longer in our plans.
You said you'd be the father of my children,
And carry my soul when I am too weak to walk.
You promised me you'll be with me forever,
And now we don't even talk.
Thought we'd be together till we were old and grey,
But street life owned your heart.
Thought we'd still be together,
But sadly, we had to part.
I remember the night you left me,
Who would have thought I wouldn't feel you
next to me another day?
Just had to get one last hustle,
Why didn't you stay?

THINK FIRST

Remember when we stood proud and tall, willing to speak up when something was wrong?
But that's when we stood together as friends and lovers, as sisters and brothers.
But now times have changed, our faces rearranged,
a message of hatred from our brothers doesn't even sound strange.
We kill for clothes, the excuse is survival.
How hard times are, when our own neighbor is our rival.
We talk about change, but nothing is done.
The message that is given is to kill, be merry, and have fun.
As I sit back and think about how life can be so insane,
a man leaves his woman to deal with all the pain,
of raising a daughter into a woman and a son into a man.
When all of our problems stem from one relationship, we were just too young to understand,
Not even equipped with the skills to survive.
So quick for change, pretended to be grown, and wound up ruining your lives,
running the streets trying to quench some ominous thirst.
My message is not to live; it is to think first.

NIGHTMARE OR SIGN?

Slipping deeper into a dream state,
heart beating fast,
Can you relate?
Running faster,
trying to escape,
the monster in my dream.
Screaming
but no one can hear,
moving faster, but
the monster stays near.
Closer it comes,
through tears I can see,
I wipe my eyes,
in a state of confusion
The Monster Was Me?

WELCOME TO AMERICA

Welcome to America, the land of the free to be ignorant and the home of I do not speak any English. Yes, welcome to the land of anything is possible, but not necessarily feasible.
Where dreams are crushed daily but people just keep on dreaming.
Where you may be added to the terrorist list if your nationality does not equal to the blonde hair blue eyed American,
Where our president reads on a fourth grade level and the fourth graders are running the household.
Welcome to the land of shaking your tail, every thing is for sale even your freedom.
Where the political dope feigns and the actual feigns, run in the same crowd.
Where living is not living, unless you're living out loud.
Welcome yes welcome to the land of freedom of speech unless it is against a nationality, race, creed, color, size, sexual preference, religious preference or disability.

Where we spend billions on nonsense but we cannot feed our poor
Where our neighbors are our enemy's, yes right next door.
The land of every one is just a little insane,
Where men women and children are called everything but there name.
Welcome to the Nation of there is no such thing as Justice
But there is a such thing as fast money, fast cars
And being happily poor, and miserably rich.

Yes welcome to America!

I pledge no allegiance on this land
In the United Sates of I'm going to get mine
And in name of the party In which it is stands
One Nation
under a groove
in suspense of reality
with suppression
and partiality for all.

Welcome to America

DEVOTED

I decided to show my love for him, exclusively devote my time and life to him, be faithful, be loyal, be all I can for him. Nevertheless, it is not just for him it is for me, see, I have never wanted us to be a he and she, Just me or just him. However, without him I could not be. See, this is not a romantic devotion. He is my God, the creator of all of things including the stars the moon and the ocean. A man that personifies all things, but what he is, is love, and he loved me, before I knew anything about him, Knew who I was before I could doubt him. Now it is all about him and the exclusive devotion I have. Some may laugh at our relationship and say it's one sided but I say for him, I would do anything because as for me I want for nothing when it comes to him. So I decided to love him exclusively and worship no other. Be faithful to him, loyal to him and show him that no one yes no one in my eyes, heart, body, and soul comes before him.

Gone

A short story about love lost

Andrew was my first love, my first kiss, my first everything. We were inseparable. For our high school yearbook, we were voted the cutest couple and the couple most likely to stay together. I was devastated to find out that we were going to different colleges; I was going to New York State, and he was going to North Carolina State. But Andrew assured me that this separation was not going to split us apart.

As planned, Andrew and I went our different ways. For the first two years, everything went fine. We stayed in touch, writing or calling each other regularly. For every break, we would meet back up in our hometown, Washington D.C., and spend all of our free time together. It seemed that the time we spent apart was bringing us closer. That was until Christmas break our sophomore year.
I was running behind, getting myself ready to go home, when my phone rang. "Rashadia." (I should have known it was going to be bad he never calls me that). "We have a change in plans this year; I am not going to be able to make it home. I have fallen behind on my studies, trying to tutor and work, so I think its best that I just stay here and catch up. I will try to make it home before the break is over."

Before he could finish I interrupted him, "Maybe I can come and keep you company and we can go home for the holidays."

"No," he said, "I need to put all my attention on my work. You know how it is when you are around me, I can't think straight. No, go home, visit your family, and I will see you soon."

I intended to argue with him, but I knew he was telling the truth. We never could study together nor do anything scholastic for that matter. While I was disappointed, I told him to hurry up and finish working so that he could come home. We said our goodbyes and I headed home.

For the first time in years, we were going to be away from each other during break. I arrived back in D.C. in time to have dinner with my family. My dad had parked my jeep in the parking garage at Union Station. While putting my stuff away in the truck, it hit me; Andrew is not going to be working 24/7, so I can go to North Carolina for a few days and whatever time he wasn't working, we could spend that time together. I spoke with my parents about what I decided to do and was on my way.

On my drive down, I called Andrew several times to tell him that I was coming, but I never got an answer. I arrived in N.C. really late so I checked into my hotel room. After I got my bags situated, I decided to try Andrew at his dorm. There was no answer, on his cell; it went straight to voicemail. I thought that was strange for his cell to be off, but I dismissed it and decided to shower and get myself something to eat.
After eating, I was exhausted but I really wanted to see him so I drove over to his dorm. Andrew had given me a key some time ago, so I let myself in. When I arrived at his room, it was already 1:00 a.m. There were a lot of packed boxes all

over the place, but I assumed his roommate was moving. After waiting for him two more hours, I decided that I would just see him tomorrow.
In the morning, I checked my phone to see if I had any missed calls; there was only one from my brother, Lawrence.

I called Andrew's phone again and received no answer, so I decided to go over there. When I arrived at his dorm, there were boxes piled up in the hallway and around his door. I got ready to open his door, but I heard voices on the other side a female and Andrew. I was immediately jealous but decided not to be immature. I reasoned with myself that he may be tutoring some dumb chick. So I used my key and opened the door. There in front of me was Andrew, naked, hugging the belly of some half-naked woman.
After throwing a half empty box at him, I stormed out of the room. I was angry; no, I was livid, hurt, and destroyed. I could not believe what I had just seen. Before I made it to my jeep, I could hear him calling for me to stop. I didn't want him to see me crying so I just kept going. Andrew was determined, and he finally caught up with me. He grabbed me and swung me around; I punched him in the face. "I deserved that," he said, "but let me explain."
"Explain what?" I asked. "How I came to see my man fully nude hugging some pregnant girl? Or how like a fool, I was loving my man and just wanting him to hold me so I drove five hours just to find that he has someone else? I do not want your explanation. You can keep that." I snatched a way my arm, continued on to my jeep, and returned to the hotel.

I packed my bags and lay down to calm my nerves, but memories of what I had just seen kept coming to me. I laid there crying, until I drifted off to sleep.

At about 2:00 p.m., I was awakened by banging on the door. "It's Andrew, Rashadia, open the door, we have to talk about this. You have to let me explain."

I opened the door, spit in his face, and slammed it again. The banging on my door continued until hotel security told him he had to leave. I immediately took a sleeping pill so that I could return to my not-so-peaceful sleep.

In the morning, I packed my jeep and checked out of the hotel. Somewhere in the midst of that I decided to do something many will deem immature and very crazy but at that point, I just didn't care.

I rode past his dorm, spotted his escalade, keyed "cheater" on both sides of it, flattened all four tires, and put sugar in his tank. I would have gotten away with it if Andrew hadn't spotted me from his dorm room window. Just as I was about to throw a brick through his windshield, Andrew grabbed my arm. "Why you got to be so immature, Shadia?"
"Why you got to be a liar?" I retorted. "I'm sorry for all that," he said. "But you don't have to be immature about this."

"Immature!!! Immature!!!" I yelled, "You are the one who cheated. I have never stepped out on you. You know what, I hate you."
He interrupted me. "I told you I could explain, but of course you don't want to hear my side of the story." I yelled, "There is nothing that you can say to me right now. Not right now. Not ever."
"Shadia, I never meant to hurt you," he told me. That was enough for me. I had heard enough and I turned to walk away. He grabbed me again, "Get off of me!" I yelled "Andrew, what did you think this was going to do to me? Were you just not going to ever tell me you have a child down here? Or were you just going to pretend that your child, and the baby's mother doesn't exist? If so, I guess it was best that I found out what kind of man you were before it was too late."

Then he blurted out, "She's my wife"

"What?" I yelled. "Oh she's your wife now, the lies continue. What else are you going to tell me, huh? That the only reason why you married her was for the baby?"

He nodded his head, yes.

"And what happened to us getting married? I know that it's out of the question now, but up until now, I had no idea that our plans changed. I came all the way down here to spend some time with my hard-working man, only to find out that not only did he start a family without me, he's married to someone else. I guess it's for the best then." I walked away from him, climbed into my jeep, and drove away.

I was so hurt by what he had done, that I immediately changed my numbers so that he couldn't reach me. All of the letters and cards that he sent me went return to sender. That was ten years ago. I returned home to D.C. after graduating Magnum Cum Laude from N.Y. State. I went on to become a lawyer working as a partner at Smith, Myers, and Smith one of the top firms in the district. Every so often, Andrew creeps into my thoughts, but I always find a way to distract myself from thinking about him.

Tonight, he showed up on my door step, begging for me to let him in, so I did. I was curios as to why, after all this time, he had shown up at my door. He came in and began apologizing for how he treated me, and for the whole situation years ago. He went on to tell me that a year after we had fallen apart, his wife and child were killed by a drunk driver who was going to be paroled this year. I started to ask him what all that had to do with me, but because I am older now and past all of the nonsense, I let him continue to talk. He went on to tell me that after his wife and child had died, he couldn't focus on finishing his degree, so he left school short of getting his Bachelors Degree in Business Management. He went on, however, to own two successful businesses and was doing well. He told me that he never loved anyone the way that he loved me. He asked me to sit. "Shadia, I mean Rashadia, I'm dying of cancer, and I couldn't leave this earth without you knowing just how much I loved you." I had no response for any of that except to tell him that he had hurt me so much that I hadn't let anyone else in those ten years. We sat around for hours rehashing the past and other things. We talked so much; we fell asleep on the couch.

In the morning, I awoke to see that he was no longer beside me. I called for him thinking that he had gone upstairs. No answer. I got up and searched the house, but he wasn't there. I came back to the living room, and noticed that there were roses all over the place. There were also two manila envelopes sitting on the coffee table. I sat down and opened the first envelope which contained a letter.

Dear Rashadia,

I enjoyed spending time with you. You have grown so much as a woman. I never thought in a million years that you would allow me to express how much I really and truly cared for you. Sadly, this is the last time that you will hear from me.

This cancer is going to kill me, but I would rather die with some dignity, so I am going to end this very soon. Enclosed in the other envelope is my last will and testament. I have left you everything that I own; you deserve it. Also, in the other envelope are the keys to my home in Decatur. It's all yours; you deserve it and so much more.

Well, I am watching you sleep and you are still as beautiful as I remembered. But I can't stay; I have to get on with my goodbyes. I love you so much.

With all my love,

Drew

My eyes filled with tears. I couldn't believe that after all these years, I was still in love him. Yet, I will never have the chance to tell him or show him just how much, for the love of my life is gone.

I hope you have enjoyed this selection. I am currently working on my novel, "Airing His Dirty laundry," and revamping another story entitled, "Cast the first stone." Again, thank you very much for supporting me. Extra Special Thank You to T.T. Martin for helping get through this without driving anyone else crazy.

Also to Steven Telesford who worked so hard on my cover and the other works of art in this selection, thank you so much for all your efforts.

Have comments about this book? Email me at loveandsuch@verizon.net or leave me comments on my personal MySpace page. www.myspace.com/poeticlyinclined

www.ingramcontent.com/pod-product-compliance
Lightning Source LLC
Chambersburg PA
CBHW022343040426
42449CB00006B/690